The

LITTLE BOOK OF
CHILLIES

THE LITTLE BOOK OF CHILLIES

Text by Emily Kearns

An Hachette UK Company
www.hachette.co.uk

Summersdale Publishers Ltd
Part of Octopus Publishing Group Limited
Carmelite House
50 Victoria Embankment
LONDON
EC4Y 0DZ
UK

www.summersdale.com

Printed and bound in Poland

ISBN: 978-1-80007-416-3

Substantial discounts on bulk quantities of Summersdale books are available to corporations, professional associations and other organizations. For details contact general enquiries: telephone: +44 (0) 1243 771107 or email: enquiries@summersdale.com.

The
LITTLE BOOK OF
CHILLIES

Rufus Cavendish

Contents

Introduction

You've no doubt picked up this book because you're partial to a chilli or two. Perhaps you prefer your chilli dishes with the heat turned up a notch, and on occasion add something a bit more fiery to your curries. You might be a grower of the humble capsicum in one or many of its forms, or a hot sauce obsessive with a penchant for testing your tolerance at chilli-eating competitions. No matter where your interest lies, there is something here for you.

There's enough to say about these little fire pods to fill *The Big Book of Chillies* – but this book is your condensed and refined selection of need-to-knows to see you on your spice journey.

We'll look at where chillies originated, how they were first used and how they have evolved to be the most-used cooking ingredient on Planet Earth. We'll ask what it is that endears so many to these brightly coloured fruits and why they burn us when we consume them.

For your education and delectation, we'll take a look at the big names in the chilli world – including the record-breaking scorchers – as well as a host of lesser-known varieties among the thousands in existence.

You will find everything you need to know in order to grow your own chillies, as well as a host of preservation ideas for when harvest time rolls around – and you can try out a number of chilli recipes too, from savoury to sweet. Whatever you do, just make sure you have a glass of milk at the ready.

THE BURNING QUESTIONS

What exactly is it that makes a chilli burn so fiercely when it comes into contact with your tongue? Why does it even have the capacity to burn? Other fruits don't behave in this way, so why do chillies? Where did these fiery pods come from in the first place and why has chilli fever blazed across the globe, scooping up a plethora of "chilli heads" who preach the wonders of the humble capsicum? How hot is the hottest chilli and what would happen if you were to eat one? The answers to those burning questions are all here. Buckle up and read on.

What are chillies?

Chillies are small, fiery, fleshy little pods that come in a seemingly never-ending procession of shapes and sizes, and a riot of vibrant colours. They belong to the Capsicum genus – part of the Solanaceae family (better known as the nightshade family) – which includes tomatoes, aubergines, potatoes and peppers. Many of us mistakenly consider chillies a vegetable. However, growing as they do from the flower of the plant, and with seeds within, they are officially a fruit. Chillies range in heat from the very mild to the explosively flavourful to the scorchingly extreme, causing many who have been brave enough (or, perhaps, foolish enough) to venture into the far end of the chilli spectrum to break a sweat and possibly shed a tear. They are one of the oldest cultivated crops in the world and are widely considered to be one of the most popular cooking ingredients globally, integral to a host of cuisines and cultures.

LITTLE RED DEVILS WITH FIRE IN THEIR SKIN AND HELL IN THEIR SEEDS.

JAMES STREET

Where did they come from?

Humans have been craving culinary heat and adding a kick to their dishes for a long, long time. Archaeologists in southern Mexico have found evidence of the use of chillies in cooking as far back as 7000 BCE and it is believed that Native Americans began to cultivate chilli plants some time after 5200 BCE. In Mexico, the Aztecs used the fiery fruit pods to make a drink called *chicahuatl,* a thick mixture of cocoa beans, corn, chillies and water that was essentially a precursor to hot chocolate. Chillies made their way to Europe via one of Christopher Columbus's ships in 1493 after he discovered them in the Caribbean and transported them back to Spain. From Spain, chilli cultivation spread across the continent like spicy wildfire, with various countries invading others and taking chillies with them, fuelling their popularity as they reached more and more cultures.

In the mid-1700s, botanist Carl Linnaeus classified the chilli as the genus *Capsicum.* From there, scientists were able to further break this down into the many varieties of chilli that are found across the globe – the main ones being *C. annuum*, *C. baccatum*, *C. chinense*, *C. frutescens* and *C. pubescens* (see page 38). Fast-forward to the present day and chillies are ubiquitous in cuisines the world over, with China the largest producer. Chillies have an enormous and dedicated following, with "chilli heads" around the world seeking an ever-more burning thrill, and enjoying a generous supply of different hot sauces, chilli festivals, competitions and events to fuel their fiery passion.

FIERY FACT

CHILLIES ARE THE MOST COMMONLY USED COOKING INGREDIENT IN THE WORLD, WITH MORE THAN A QUARTER OF THE GLOBAL POPULATION EATING THEM DAILY.

WHAT IS NOT TO LOVE ABOUT THE HOT AND SPICY? THERE IS SOMETHING ALLURING IN THE THRILL OF THE SPICY BUZZ, THE ZING THAT TRAVELS UP AND DOWN YOUR TONGUE, THE TINGLING OF THE TASTE BUDS WHEN YOU EAT HOT AND SPICY FOOD.

MIKE AND PATTY
HULTQUIST

What makes chillies hot?

When it comes to chilli heat, we've all bitten off more than we can chew at one point or another – whether we've proceeded knowingly into the realms of fiery cuisine, ordered outside our comfort zone in a restaurant, been served something our tongue simply couldn't handle or daringly popped a whole Carolina Reaper into our mouth. We all know that creeping feeling as the burn takes over and our taste buds go on strike. This is down to the chemical compounds found in chillies called capsaicinoids – the most common being capsaicin. Capsaicin is the culprit when it comes to intensity of a chilli. Officially a chemical irritant, it will cause a burning sensation in any tissue it comes in contact with – for example, your mouth, stomach, skin or eyes (if you've been that unlucky).

What is the science behind chilli heat?

When you eat a chilli, capsaicin is released into your saliva. It then binds itself to the TRPV1 receptors – also known as capsaicin receptors – the function of which is to detect extreme heat in your mouth, alerting your brain to the fact that you're consuming something fiery. Once the receptors have been triggered they send signals to your brain telling it that your mouth is ablaze and needs neutralizing. The brain then responds by attempting to cool the body down – hence the onset of watering eyes, a running nose and even sweating. Chillies evolved this brain-tricking chemical to stop them from being consumed by mammals and to allow birds, which do not experience the burning sensation, to liberally sprinkle their seeds throughout nature and allow propagation. However, little did the chillies know that humans would grow to worship the burn and would only want more.

Why do we love the burn?

Chillies fall into the reasonably small category of foods that offer something at the moment of eating that lies beyond taste or smell. Think about the cool and refreshing sensation experienced when biting into a new piece of gum, sucking a strong mint or eating mint-choc-chip ice cream; or the so-called "chewy" tannins and particular "mouthfeel" in certain classes of red wine or tea; or how about the effervescent, popping attack of a fizzy drink as it glides over your tongue? Chillies raise the temperature and bring on the heat sensation, which, when it gets really intense, can feel like pain. As we've discussed, this is really all down to the receptors in your mouth telling your brain that things have hotted up somewhat – no damage is actually being done.

The effect of the heat sensation raises our heartbeat and triggers the release of endorphins – our bodies' natural painkillers – causing us to feel happy and relaxed. This rush of pleasure is one of the reasons chilli lovers keep coming back for more, and it explains the growing numbers of thrill-seekers chasing ever-hotter varieties. Much like the adrenaline hit that comes from rollercoasters or extreme sports, the chilli rush comes from the fact that eating one is a "constrained risk" – it provides all the fun of a risk with little to none of the danger, and it fuels the participant to go back for more. The more we consume chillies, the more tolerant we become of their firepower and the more we feel the need for a hotter hit. Eating chillies every day could quickly turn you into a fire-breathing chilli head with a taste for the extreme, because you'll be able to handle the heat with far greater ease than you could before.

FIERY FACT

JAPANESE SAMURAI WOULD EAT
CHILLI PEPPERS BEFORE GOING
INTO BATTLE, IN ORDER TO HELP
THEM FEEL INVINCIBLE.

FOR THE TRUE CULINARY
THRILL-SEEKER, HABANEROS
ARE THE KING OF STING.

VICKI MATTERN

What's the best way to cool your mouth down?

After passing your heat limit you might start to feel rising discomfort and need something to stem the mouth fire. It might feel natural to reach for a glass of cold water – it's how you'd put out a physical fire, so why not cool the burning within your body the same way? You can try, but it won't do very much as capsaicin doesn't dissolve in water. Try reaching for a glass of milk instead. Tried and tested methods find the best cure for spice overload is something from the dairy spectrum. Think milk, yoghurt or – a favourite among many chilli heads – vanilla ice cream. Dairy products contain the protein casein, which does a great job of breaking down the oil-based capsaicin molecules that have well and truly bound themselves to the receptors in your mouth, and the colder they are, the more they will soothe the scorching sensation. Wilbur Scoville himself (see page 26) was one of the first people to propose milk as an antidote to chilli burn.

Where in the world do chillies grow?

According to Guinness World Records, when the numbers rolled in at the end of 2018, China was by far the world's biggest producer of chillies, racking up a whopping 45 per cent of global production. The Food and Agriculture Organization of the United Nations estimates the annual global production of chillies to be 40.9 million tonnes – imagine the heat. Although China produces the most chillies, Mexico exports more – with an impressive $1.4 billion (£1.11 billion) in exports in 2019 compared with China's $97.3 million (£77.3 million).

THE WORLD'S TOP CHILLI PRODUCERS

COUNTRY	CHILLIES PRODUCED IN 2018
China	8.54 million tonnes
Mexico	3.44 million tonnes
Turkey	2.56 million tonnes

What is the hottest part of a chilli?

Contrary to popular belief, the hottest part of the chilli is not the seeds but the placenta – the fleshy white strip that runs down the centre of the fruit and to which the seeds are attached. To lessen the impact of a chilli, make sure you remove the seeds and the placenta. The mildest part of the chilli is known as the apex and can be found at the tip.

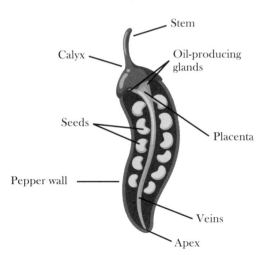

Stem

Calyx

Oil-producing glands

Seeds

Placenta

Pepper wall

Veins

Apex

FIERY FACT

THE WORD "CHILLI" COMES FROM THE NAHUATL LANGUAGE, WHICH IS SPOKEN IN THE HIGHLANDS OF MEXICO.

How is a chilli's heat measured?

If you're partial to a bit of chilli heat, it's likely you'll have heard of the Scoville scale. But you might be interested to know its origin and how exactly it measures the burn of a chilli pepper. The scale was developed in 1912 by American pharmacist Wilbur Scoville. He had a notion to crack the capsaicin heat conundrum, and his legacy now gives chilli heads the world over something to measure their conquests against. Scoville set about quantifying the hotness of a chilli by dissolving a small, specific amount of chilli extract in sugar water. Assisted by a team of human tasters, he continued to dilute the extract until the burn could no longer be detected. The more a chilli extract had to be diluted, the hotter the chilli and the higher the rating of Scoville heat units (SHU) it received.

However, human error was a major factor – we don't all have taste buds that function in exactly the same way, and some of us are likely to be more sensitive to chilli heat than others. In time, Scoville's methods were overhauled, and these days things are a little more scientific and a little less reliant on human guinea pigs. Scientists use a process known as high-performance liquid chromatography (HPLC) – which separates, identifies and quantifies each component in a mixture – to measure the chilli's capsaicin content, and a Scoville rating is awarded based on their findings. This makes the chilli unique, as no other fruit has its own system of measurement.

What are the hottest chillies in the world?

Chilli obsessives in the business of breeding new varieties are forever chasing the ultimate gong – hottest chilli in the world. The coveted accolade is currently held by the Carolina Reaper, which snatched the title in 2013 and has held on to the top spot ever since – even surpassing its own record in 2021 to reach a higher Scoville rating than ever before. Though it now languishes at number 10, the Red Savina Habanero held the title from 1994 to 2006 with a hearty 500,000 SHU – before chilli fever well and truly took hold and the world started chasing chillies at the face-meltingly hot end of the scale.

CHILLI	SCOVILLE HEAT UNITS
Carolina Reaper	1,500,000–2,200,000
Trinidad Moruga Scorpion	1,500,000–2,009,231
7 Pot Douglah	1,000,000–1,853,936
7 Pot Primo	1,100,000–1,469,000
Trinidad Scorpion "Butch T"	800,000–1,463,700
Naga Viper	600,000–1,382,118
7 Pot Barrackpore	900,000–1,300,000
7 Pot Red (Giant)	500,000–1,100,000
Ghost Pepper (Bhut Jolokia)	600,000–1,041,427
Red Savina Habanero	250,000–577,000

Hot or not?

How far have you travelled up the Scoville scale? Use this handy guide to plan your next step up.

CAROLINA REAPER: 2,200,000

TRINIDAD MORUGA SCORPION: 2,009,231

GHOST PEPPER (BHUT JOLOKIA): 1,041,427

HABANERO: 577,000

SCOTCH BONNET: 325,000

BIRD'S EYE: 225,000

CAYENNE: 50,000

JALAPEÑO: 8,000

BELL PEPPER: 0

FIERY FACT

DESPITE THEIR DISTINCTIVE FLAVOURS, THE JALAPEÑO AND CHIPOTLE CHILLI COME FROM THE SAME PLANT – CHIPOTLE IS THE DRIED VERSION OF THE SPICY GREEN BULLET.

Why are chillies so popular?

In countries such as India, Mexico, Thailand and China, chillies have been vital to everyday dishes for many years. As these countries' cuisines have become more well-known in other parts of the world, appreciation of the chilli has grown in a big way.

It's safe to say chillies are the only fruit that can boast a global fan base numbering millions upon millions. These so-called "chilli heads" take their appreciation for the fiery pod beyond mere culinary enjoyment, and dedicate their time and energy to seeking out ever-hotter varieties, as well as attending related festivals, events and conventions. That'll be the endorphin rush again and the living-on-the-edge-although-not-quite experience one feels upon chowing down on a Carolina Reaper or two.

The chilli fever that swept the rest of the globe is a phenomenon that started to really emerge in the 1980s and 1990s, as different cuisines were given a global stage and people started to realize chillies were something to get excited about. More than just heat, they offered a wide range of incredible flavours and could transform the way people cooked.

This trend has only exploded in more recent years, with the internet giving these mega-fans a voice – and a YouTube account – allowing them to share tasting notes and challenge members of their heat-loving community to step further into the inferno.

Are chillies good for you?

You might be surprised to know chillies add far more to our diets than a spicy kick. They are a veritable superfood, packed as they are with:

- **Vitamin A** – dried chillies are rich in vitamin A (containing more than carrots), which we require to maintain healthy tissues of the gastrointestinal, reproductive and respiratory tracts.

- **Vitamin C** – chillies contain more vitamin C than oranges, with the highest levels being found in ripe red chillies.

- **Vitamin D** – chillies contain such high levels of vitamin D that some athletes swear by consuming chillies before training in order to prevent injury.

- **Potassium** – chillies are high in potassium, with green varieties containing even more than red. Potassium helps us to maintain regular levels of fluid in our blood cells.

- **Calcium** – within the humble chilli you'll also find calcium, a mineral which allows us to maintain healthy bones and teeth, and plays a role in heart and nerve functions, blood clotting and muscle contraction.

- **Beta-carotene** – hot peppers are rich in beta-carotene, which converts to vitamin A in the body.

- **Antioxidants** – cultures in which chillies feature heavily have lower rates of cancer, heart disease and diabetes thanks to the humble chilli's antioxidants.

Chillies may go some way to help prevent diabetes, cancer and heart disease, treat arthritis and ease congestion. They can also boost your metabolism and increase the oxidation of fat, both of which promote healthy weight loss. Research has also shown they can help to protect your stomach lining – which might not be your first thought after a particularly hot curry.

THE BIG NAMES

From the punchy jalapeños scattered across your mountain of nachos, to the fiery bird's eyes lurking in your Thai curry, to the sweet, salty, pan-fried Padróns on your tapas tabletop, chillies are ubiquitous in global cuisines – and many of us are privileged to enjoy them wherever we are in the world. Whether you prefer to turn up the heat and break a sweat while you chow down or would rather savour sweet, fruity and mild chilli flavours, there is something of every heat for every palate. Here we delve into the wheres, whats and hows of the most famous chillies out there and throw in a healthy helping of interesting, lesser-known names to whet your appetite.

Chilli species

While the chilli species in existence are too numerous to mention, there are five that are commonly grown, from which more than 3,000 different varieties have emerged.

- *Capsicum annuum:* This is the most common species and includes varieties such as cayenne, jalapeño and pimento. Capsicum annuum chillies are predominantly grown in China, the Caribbean, India and Mexico, and tend to range in heat from zero to 125,000 SHU.

- *Capsicum baccatum:* These small, berry-like chillies are the most widely grown in South America, as they love to bask in the hot sun. Better known as Aji chillies, these are celebrated for their fruity, smoky taste and tend to range in heat from 3,000 to 30,000 SHU.

- *Capsicum chinense:* These are the hottest chillies around, and include varieties such as the Scotch bonnet, habanero and notorious Carolina Reaper.

Hot and fruity, and most widely grown across the Caribbean, the fieriest chillies in the world fall into this species and range in heat from 100,000 to an almighty 2.2 million SHU.

- *Capsicum frutescens*: These chillies are small but fiery, packing a heat-fuelled punch despite their size. Varieties in this species include the tabasco and piri-piri chillies, and their heat ranges from 50,000 to 225,000 SHU.

- *Capsicum pubescens*: Better known as Rocoto chillies in Peru and Ecuador, and Manzano chillies in Mexico, these varieties are fleshier than their scorching siblings and are set apart by their black seeds. The plants grow in cooler temperatures than other varieties, and their firepower builds all the way from zero to 75,000 SHU.

Pimiento de Padrón

Species: *Capsicum annuum*
Also known as: Herbón
Heat level: 🌶
Scoville units: 500–2,500

More commonly referred to as Padrón peppers, these made their way from South America to Padrón in Galicia, Spain, in 1600s, where they were reinvented and quickly became prevalent in the country's cuisine. If you've ever frequented a tapas restaurant or holidayed in Spain, you've no doubt munched on several of these shiny green delights pan-fried and sprinkled with salt – and you'll also know that while these peppers are generally sweet and mild, around one in eight can be hotter than you might expect. If left to mature, the Padrón will turn red, but the pepper we know and love is always harvested while green. Although they're now widely grown across other parts of the Mediterranean and the United States, Padrón peppers are inextricably tied to Spanish food and culture, with the Festival de Pimiento de Padrón held in Galicia annually to celebrate the much-loved delicacy.

Pimento

Species: *Capsicum annuum*
Types: Perfection, floral gem, super red
Heat level: 🌶
Scoville units: 500–1,000

The pimento (or pimiento) has much in common with the humble red pepper, sporting the same familiar heart shape and vibrant red skin. This mild and sweet chilli pepper is grown in huge numbers and sold commercially – often pickled and stuffed into olives or ground down to become one of the main ingredients in paprika. Also known as the "cherry pepper", the pimento hails from South America but is now widely grown in warm European countries and the Middle East. While the pimento is a specific chilli pepper, its name actually just means "pepper" in Spanish.

Poblano

Species: *Capsicum annuum*
Types: Ancho (dried variety)
Heat level: 🌶
Scoville units: 1,000–2,000

These proud, glossy deep-green fruits are heart-shaped, mild and best served stuffed and roasted. Originating in Puebla, Mexico, what they lack in heat they make up for in flavour, packing a strong, peppery punch. The most popular chilli in Mexican cuisine, the poblano is another that will ripen to a dark red or brown if left unpicked, but is nearly always harvested while green. Find them on the menu in every Mexican restaurant, often stuffed with cheese, battered and deep fried. Dried poblanos become the sweet and chocolatey ancho, which is sold either whole, flaked or ground, and is a vital ingredient in Mexican and Tex-Mex marinades and sauces.

FIERY FACT

BEFORE THE SPANISH CONQUEST, THE MAYANS USED CHILLIES FOR PROTECTION FROM THEIR ENEMIES – BURNING ROWS OF THEM TO CREATE A PUNGENT AND INVASIVE SMOKESCREEN.

LIFE ISN'T LIKE A BOX OF
CHOCOLATES. IT'S MORE LIKE
A JAR OF JALAPEÑOS. WHAT
YOU DO TODAY MIGHT BURN
YOUR BUTT TOMORROW.

DANIEL LAWRENCE WHITNEY
(LARRY THE CABLE GUY)

Jalapeño

Species: *Capsicum annuum*
Types: Gigantia, early, tam mild, sweet
Heat level:
Scoville units: 2,500–8,000

The jalapeño is a household name, rising to fame along with the popularity of Mexican cuisine. We know it as the little green (often pickled) pepper, but it can grow up to 12 cm (4 ½ in.) long, and, although we are accustomed to consuming it when green, it is actually red when fully ripened. With its history rooted firmly in Mexican soil, the jalapeño can be traced back to the Aztecs who pioneered its culinary use before the Spanish conquest. Jalapeños account for a whopping 30 per cent of chilli production in Mexico and, in more recent years, are grown in huge numbers in California, New Mexico and Texas. The traditional Mexican method of drying jalapeños is how we have come to know and love the smoky chipotle, giving us a new level of appreciation for this chilli.

Species: *Capsicum annuum*

Types: Serrano del sol, fire, giant, purple

Heat level: 🌶️ 🌶️

Scoville units: 10,000–25,000

This bullet-shaped red chilli erupts from a plant with distinctive furry leaves. Its Spanish name, "*serrano*", means "from the mountains", which gives you an idea of this variety's birthplace – the mountain ridges of Puebla and Hidalgo in Mexico. The second most used chilli in Mexican cuisine, following the poblano, the serrano chilli is fleshier than some of its fiery counterparts, making it ideal for pico de gallo and salsas. While we typically know this chilli to be red in colour once ripe, it can also vary to green, brown, orange and yellow.

Cayenne

Species: *Capsicum annuum*
Types: Dagger pod, golden, Carolina
Heat level: 🌶️🌶️
Scoville units: 30,000–50,000

Named after the capital of French Guiana, the cayenne is what you would draw to illustrate a chilli to visitors from another planet who had not come across this fiery fruit before. Long and red, tapering to a sharp point, the cayenne can reach up to 20 cm (8 in.) in length and is a popular addition to Indian and Chinese dishes – especially Szechuan sauces in the latter. Medical research is purported to have found health benefits in the humble cayenne due to its anticoagulant properties – which help to thin the blood – and it is also thought to have a hand in increasing metabolism. Native Americans have also been using cayenne to treat stomach aches, indigestion and circulation issues for thousands of years.

Habanero

Species: *Capsicum chinense*
Types: Red, brown, chocolate-brown, orange, mustard, paper lantern, big sun, red savina
Heat level: 🌶🌶🌶
Scoville units: 100,000–577,000

The habanero is a heat-bringing favourite that adds quite a kick to dishes and sauces. Habanero means "from Havana" (*La Habana*), so named because it was once traded there – although, perhaps surprisingly, it is not commonly used in Cuban cuisine. Originally hailing from the Amazon, the habanero travelled north and found favour in Mexico. Now, most of its production takes place on the Yucatán Peninsula, but you'll also find it growing in Belize, Colombia, Costa Rica, Ecuador, Panama and in several US states. This innocent-looking Chinese-lantern-shaped chilli pepper packs an almighty punch and should be used sparingly depending on your heat tolerance. The habanero is known for its sneaky heat-building properties, with its effect on your mouth likely to grow over the space of a few minutes and last for up to an hour.

Bird's eye

Species: *Capsicum annuum*
Also known as: pequin, peri-peri, Thai, tiny chilli
Heat level: 🌶 🌶 🌶
Scoville units: 100,000–225,000

This red chilli may be tiny but its heat is huge, as is its sweet and peppery flavour. While it is prevalent in Southeast Asian cuisine – particularly in Thailand, where it is used extensively in curries, soups and marinades – the bird's eye actually hails from Africa and is still known to grow wild in Ethiopia. It is not unusual for a single small plant to be incredibly productive and yield hundreds of these tiny chillies.

FIERY FACT

EAT THE JAPANESE CHILLI SHISHITO AND YOU'LL FIND YOURSELF PLAYING A TYPE OF PEPPER ROULETTE – THESE CHILLIES ARE USUALLY MILD, BUT ABOUT ONE IN TEN WILL BE REALLY QUITE SPICY.

HABANEROS ARE PURE HEAT.
THEY ARE A SMALL, ORANGE
LANTERN-SHAPED CHILLI
THAT SHOULD BE HANDLED
WITH RESPECT, IF NOT
DOWNRIGHT SUSPICION.

MARY SUE MILLIKEN

Scotch bonnet

Species: *Capsicum chinense*
Types: Scotch bonnet red, big sun,
Burkina yellow
Heat level: 🌶🌶🌶
Scoville units: 125,000–325,000

The Scotch bonnet is the habanero's Caribbean cousin, closely related but with a sweeter flavour and sporting a squatter, less delicate shape – less Chinese lantern and more Scottish tam-o'-shanter, which is of course how this fiery number got its name. Prevalent in cuisine across the Caribbean and West Africa, the Scotch bonnet is a vital ingredient in sauces, marinades and barbecue seasoning and brings a distinctive flavour to traditional jerk dishes. Sometimes known as the Caribbean red or bonney pepper, its roots can be traced back to the jungles of the western Amazon basin, before it made its way to Jamaica and was embraced and adopted as something of a national treasure.

Carolina Reaper

Species: *Capsicum chinense*
Types: Moruga scorpion, Moruga brainstrain
Heat level: 🌶🌶🌶🌶🌶
Scoville units: 1,500,000–2,200,000

In 2013, the Carolina Reaper was crowned the world's hottest chilli pepper by Guinness World Records. This devilish inferno was the brainchild of Ed Currie, founder of the aptly named PuckerButt Pepper Company in South Carolina and known to many as "Smokin' Ed". The Carolina Reaper is a cross-breed between the Caribbean La Soufrière and Pakistani naga viper chillies and is so-named "reaper" for its scorpion-like tail. Its sweet, fruity flavour will quickly give way to a cascade of fire in your mouth and an unholy burning sensation – or "molten lava" as it is sometimes described. Currie's world-beating creation continues to outperform even itself every year, with 2021 seeing its Scoville rating surpass the previously recorded figure to reach new levels of hellfire.

Honourable mentions

Here are a select few of the more interesting, fearsome, widely used and lesser-known varieties across the chilli spectrum.

BHUT JOLOKIA

Species: *Capsicum chinense*

Scoville units: 600,000–1,041,427

More commonly known as the "ghost pepper", the bhut jolokia comes from India and is one of the hottest chillies in the world. Unique in shape – bulbous with fine, crumpled skin – the fruits ripen from green to orange to red and offer only the bravest chilli connoisseur an extreme sensory experience.

BRAZILIAN STARFISH

Species: *Capsicum baccatum*

Scoville units: 15,000–20,000

These beautiful starfish-shaped chillies grow on vines and originally hail from Peru, although they are now cultivated in Brazil. Sweet, fruity and vibrant red, with a healthy level of heat, the starfish is a popular ornamental pepper as well as one for foodies and chilli heads.

FACING HEAVEN

Species: *Capsicum chinense*

Scoville units: 10,000–50,000

These conical red chillies grow to around 8–10 cm and point skywards, hence the name. They come from Sichuan province in China and you'll find them in many of the country's popular dishes. Upon eating, expect an intense heat that mellows to a slow burn.

JAMAICAN HOT CHOCOLATE

Species: *Capsicum chinense*

Scoville units: 100,000–200,000

These chillies from the Caribbean are hot, strong and smoky. Related to the habanero and Scotch bonnet, they are similar in shape, darkening to a deep chocolate brown when ripe.

MANZANO

Species: *Capsicum pubescens*

Scoville units: 30,000–50,000

One of the few South American chillies that doesn't belong to the *C. annuum* species, the manzano is shaped like a little apple and will ripen to yellow, orange or red, depending on the type.

NAGA VIPER

Species: *Capsicum chinense*

Scoville units: 600,000–1,382,118

The work of chilli breeder Gerard Fowler in the Lake District, UK, this super-hot chilli is the product of fusing the Trinidad Moruga scorpion, naga morich and ghost pepper.

PEPPADEW 🌶

Species: *Capsicum annuum*

Scoville units: 1,000–1,200

While the origins of the peppadew are unknown, the chilli was discovered by Johan Steenkamp in the garden of his holiday home on the Eastern Cape in South Africa, who then rolled it out commercially on a grand scale. The peppers are cherry-tomato-sized and sweet, and are delicious pickled.

POT BLACK 🌶 🌶

Species: *Capsicum annuum*

Scoville units: 30,000–50,000

These glossy, black, bullet-shaped fruits are striking – and even more so when seen on the plant which has black-tinted leaves and stems and purple flowers. Although they eventually ripen to a deep scarlet, they are usually picked black and pack some serious firepower and an intense flavour.

PRAIRIE FIRE

Species: *Capsicum annuum*

Scoville units: 70,000–80,000

Produced from an attractive, ornamental chilli plant that produces hundreds of fruits, this chilli gets its name from the ripening stages – from yellow, to orange, to deep red. An ideal kitchen-windowsill addition for both aesthetic purposes and for adding a kick when cooking.

ROCOTILLO

Species: *Capsicum chinense*

Scoville units: 1,500–2,500

These small, bell-shaped peppers are a relative of the habanero and Scotch bonnet, but are far milder. Hailing from the Caribbean, they ripen to orange, brown or red, have a distinctive, sweet flavour, and are widely used in jerk marinades and dishes.

TABASCO

Species: *Capsicum frutescens*

Scoville units: 30,000–50,000

Predominantly grown on Avery Island, Louisiana, USA – home to the famous Tabasco sauce factory since 1868 – this chilli pepper is synonymous with hot sauce. Smoky and hot, with a good old kick, the tabasco chilli is hotter than the much-loved sauce, which is thought to clock in at around 5,000 SHU.

TRINIDAD MORUGA SCORPION

Species: *Capsicum chinense*

Scoville units: 1,500,000–2,009,231

Verging on surface-of-the-sun hot, this is a glove-wearing affair. It's literally too hot to handle and is only surpassed in heat by the Carolina Reaper. Those who have eaten one raw have described the slow-building sensation of a fire growing from within their body. The thought alone is enough to make the eyes water.

HERE,
THERE AND
EVERYWHERE

It's time to talk hot sauce – the conduit for a chilli revolution that has inspired and fired up a global following for the humble capsicum; a movement with fans so devout they dedicate themselves to both creating and seeking out the hottest condiments known to man. Here you will also learn about growing these little fire pockets, what it entails, how easy it is, where you can do it and what to do with the end product. We're talking drying, crushing, pickling, smoking and more. You will never want for chillies again. We'll also hear about the reigning chilli-eating champion of the world and the techniques she swears by to get to the fiery finish, not to mention other uses for this wondrous fruit – from the medicinal to the protective. It's all here.

Some like it hot

Hot sauce, it's fair to say, has a similarly loyal and excitable following as the chillies themselves. Much like the craft beer movement, since the turn of the century hot sauce has exploded in popularity, with anyone and everyone attempting to create something new and different. The market is completely saturated; specialist shops display shelf upon shelf of little red, brown, yellow and green bottles boasting their provenance, backstory and trendy packaging – so much so that it can begin to feel overwhelming!

To understand the phenomenon we should go back to the beginning. The earliest known hot sauce was created by the Aztecs, who ground chillies and herbs into water in order to make their food more flavourful – and sometimes to use as a form of punishment (ouch).

Hot sauce wasn't commercialized until the early 1800s; preserved newspaper adverts from Massachusetts, USA, show early examples of cayenne pepper sauces being sold. However, no evidence is required for the hot sauce that emerged in the 1870s, when Edmund McIlhenny founded the McIlhenny Company on Avery Island in Louisiana, USA, and developed a recipe for Tabasco. This household-name spicy red sauce was developed using vinegar, chillies and salt as an antidote to the bland food of the American South at the time. McIlhenny grew his own chillies – tabasco, of course – on Avery Island and acquired a patent for the sauce in 1870. By the end of the decade his sauce was being sold across the United States and Europe. The branding and packaging of the iconic diminutive glass bottle, with a green paper collar and red top, has barely changed in the past century, and Tabasco sauce is still made using the chilli crop from Avery Island. Well, if it ain't broke...

Some like it hotter

In the 1980s another household-name chilli sauce was born. David Tran's Huy Fong Foods originated following his family's migration from Vietnam to California aboard a freighter of the same name. As the Southeast Asian immigrant population grew in the Golden State, Tran decided to furnish them with home comforts in the shape of the hot sauce he used to make back home. He sold it in baby-food jars from the back of his van, and the sweet, hot, red liquid we know as sriracha was born. The bottle and branding remain unchanged from the early days – featuring the iconic rooster that represents the year of Tran's birth – and the rest, as they say, is history.

Things were hotting up in the chilli sauce arena as more and more people succumbed to chilli fever. In the 1980s the first dedicated hot sauce shop, Le Saucier, opened in Boston and the 1990s saw the introduction of superhot chillies, which, in turn, led to the inception of blow-your-head-off sauce variants, such as the famous Blair's Death Sauce.

By 2020, the hot sauce industry was estimated to be worth an astonishing $2.54 billion (£2.03 billion), and, with a projected worth of $4.38 billion (£3.49 billion) by 2028, it's expected to thrive well into the future.

FIERY FACT

IN 1932, THE UK GOVERNMENT
BANNED THE SALE OF TABASCO SAUCE
DURING A "BUY BRITISH" CAMPAIGN.
MEMBERS OF PARLIAMENT MADE SUCH A
FUSS THAT THEIR PROTESTS WERE DUBBED
"THE TABASCO TEMPEST" AND PARLIAMENT
WAS FORCED TO ALLOW THE SALE OF THE
BELOVED HOT SAUCE ONCE MORE.

Keep your powder dry

It's not just about fresh chillies and hot sauces; chilli powder and paprika are some of the most used cooking ingredients in the world. These two spices differ in that chilli powder is usually a blend of pulverized chillies and a variety of other spices, whereas paprika is truer to its pure red chilli roots.

Abundant throughout Hungarian cuisine to this day, paprika made an early appearance in the country in the 1500s before being adopted by Western cuisines in the 1900s. Its vivid red hue brings colour as well as flavour to dishes, and it can also be sprinkled on top of foods as a garnish.

And let's not forget cayenne pepper, which is another popular pulverized chilli ingredient, bringing the heat to cuisines far and wide.

Sugar and spice

To the untrained taste bud, chilli and chocolate might sound like a revolting combination – like strawberries and sauerkraut or bananas and horseradish, or, indeed, like chalk and cheese. Chilli and chocolate sounds like a fad – something to be found on a modern menu striving for difference and column inches – but in fact it dates back a long, long way.

Thousands of years ago, the Aztecs were mixing cocoa beans, chillies, corn and water together to make the precursor to hot chocolate. It worked then and it works now. And people have long been adding a square or two of dark chocolate to their chilli con carne in order to give it more body. Chocolate with a kick is a taste sensation beloved by foodies all over – and with good reason, as it adds a new dimension to your dessert. Turn to pages 119 and 121 to give chilli chocolate cheesecake and chilli chocolate brownies a whirl.

FIERY FACT

PLENTY OF PEOPLE GROW ORNAMENTAL
CHILLI PEPPERS IN THEIR GARDENS
TO BRING VIBRANT COLOURS TO THEIR
BORDERS. WHILE THESE PEPPERS ARE
EDIBLE, SOME TEND TO BE ALL ABOUT STYLE
OVER SUBSTANCE AND WON'T BRING MUCH
FLAVOUR TO YOUR TABLE.

Grow your own

Growing your own chillies is pretty simple and, if well cared for, plants can bear an abundance of fruit. It's a good idea to start early if you plan to grow chillies from seed – work towards sowing seeds in winter if you have a heated propagator, or in early spring if you're simply relying on a sunny windowsill.

Once your seedlings have sprouted, transfer them to slightly larger pots and allow leaves to develop. Then transfer them to bigger pots (30 cm will do) filled with peat-free compost to allow them to reach their full potential. As the weather grows warmer, move the chilli plants outside. Chillies like to be warm, so, if you want them to brighten up the garden, make sure they're in a sunny spot. Bring them inside come autumn to keep them safe from the chill of winter.

THINGS TO REMEMBER

🌶 Chillies need watering regularly, but be careful not to overwater them as this can reduce their heat. Err on the dry side rather than potentially giving them too much water but keep the soil damp. Keep a watchful eye in hot weather as they may need to be watered daily.

🌶 Make sure the plants have plenty of support – staking helps to keep your plants upright when they bear lots of fruit. Larger varieties of pepper, such as poblano, will become especially heavy once the chillies begin to show.

🌶 As well as watering your plants, make sure you're giving them plant feed weekly – tomato fertilizer will do the job.

🌶 Before transferring plants from the house to the garden, put them outside during the day for about a week so they can acclimatize.

🌶 When chillies appear, pick the first few before they turn red. This will encourage the plant to produce more, which you can then leave to ripen.

How's it hanging?

If your outside space is limited, why not try growing chillies in a hanging basket? As well as being a great space-saver, once your plant bears fruit it will also look quite beautiful and brighten up your surroundings.

YOU WILL NEED:

Hanging basket
Liner
Circle to fit your basket cut from thick plastic bag
Compost
Compact chilli seedling – prairie fire works well

First of all, place your liner in the hanging basket and make sure it's flush with the edges.

Add the plastic to the bottom of the basket and add compost until it is two-thirds full.

Plant the chilli seedling in the middle and press down the compost firmly, then fill the rest of the space with compost and water it.

Water your basket regularly and give the plant tomato feed once a week.

As soon as your chillies appear and ripen, get picking!

TOP TIP: If you sow spring onion and coriander seeds around the edges of your chilli plant, not only will you be making use of all the space, but you will also have much of what you need for a delicious salsa – all in one basket.

Preserving chillies

If your chilli growing is successful it's likely there will be a glut of fruit come harvest time. Don't feel you have to eat them all at once! There are many different ways you can preserve your crop to enjoy later – from pickling to drying, freezing or smoking. You can even make your own chilli flakes and chilli-infused oils to sprinkle and drizzle over anything you fancy. This is especially ideal for those who like to keep a variety of chilli plants, whether it's for their ornamental value or for the purpose of having a host of different heats available on demand. With the following methods you can make sure no fire pod goes to waste and that there are always plenty of gifts for the chilli lovers in your life.

Feeling chilli?

A quick and easy way to deal with an abundance of chillies is to freeze them. This takes the least amount of effort and is ideal if you're looking to preserve their freshness. First, make sure the chillies you want to freeze are ripe and fresh. Then, wash and dry them thoroughly and freeze them in a container or bag. Another option to help speed up meal preparation is to slice the chillies and freeze them along with some water in an ice-cube tray. When you need some chopped chillies, voila; simply pop an ice cube into whatever it is you're cooking. If you'd rather cut out the water, slice the chillies and place them on a baking tray in the freezer for 3 hours before removing and transferring them to a container. Keep the container in the freezer and shake out a small amount of chilli slices whenever you need them.

Crisp and dry

There are several ways to dry your chillies – both practical and decorative – so, if you have a bumper crop, this could be the solution for you. Most chillies can be dried, but some fare better than others. Opt for thinner, less fleshy chillies, such as cayenne, as these will dry much more quickly and will crush well, and always wash your chillies beforehand.

If you are blessed with a warm climate, you can live the chilli dream and dry them outside in the sunshine. Either lay them out on trays in the direct heat of the sun or, if they have long stems, bunch them up and hang them in a warm, sunny spot. You may even find that smaller, thinner chillies will dry on a sunny windowsill.

Oven-drying chillies is a good idea if you'd like to dry lots at once. Line baking trays with greaseproof paper and spread the chillies out on top. Place in the oven at 100°C (210°F) and check on them regularly until they are suitably shrivelled. If the chillies snap easily, they are ready. The key is to get the oven to a heat that won't burn the chillies but will instead remove their moisture. Leave the oven door open slightly if you're worried about scorching them.

If you're enthusiastic about drying chillies, you might want to invest in a dehydrator. This will make the process very simple and you will be able to use your new tech to dry all sorts of other foods too. Drying some of your harvest will allow you to really get the most out of your chillies because, in dried form, their flavour deepens, becoming richer and hotter.

Get crushing

Once your chillies are suitably dry (see page 76) you can get crushing. It's worth doing this a few chillies at a time and only crushing more once this supply has run out. Dried chillies retain their oils better when whole, so you'll only want to have as many chilli flakes as you will use within a couple of weeks.

FLAKES

Crushing your chillies is simple. Remove the stalks and throw them into a food processor – but stop pulsing once they are coarsely ground. You want the end result to be a pile of vibrant flakes. Alternatively, grab a pestle and mortar and use some elbow grease – and you might want to sport a face mask while crushing in this way to avoid chilli-burn in your airways! Store your chilli flakes in an airtight container.

POWDER

You can also grind your dried chillies to make your own chilli powder, which is incredibly satisfying. For this you will need a spice mill or a coffee grinder – but it's unlikely you'll want to use the coffee grinder for its intended purpose again so think carefully before you reach for this. You will want to wear a face mask to avoid inhaling any of the powder and perhaps even some goggles (swimming or skiing goggles will do if you have nothing else to hand!) to protect your eyes. This is particularly important if you are crushing superhot varieties of chilli. Once you have achieved a fine powder consistency, store in an airtight container.

Pick some pickled peppers

Pickling your chillies is a great way to make full use of an abundant crop. It's incredibly easy to do and won't take much time, and it doesn't matter what type of chilli you're growing – nearly all will preserve well. Here's your handy guide to pickling:

INGREDIENTS:

(Based on one medium-sized jar)

150 g fresh chillies of your choice
250 ml wine or cider vinegar
80 ml water
2 tbsp sugar
1 tsp salt
1 clove garlic

- Make sure your jars are sterilized – you can do this by filling them with freshly boiled water and leaving them for 30 minutes. Sterilize your jars as close to pickling time as possible and make sure they are still warm when you transfer the chillies.

🌶 Wash your chillies well and dry them so they are not dripping wet. Add the vinegar, water and sugar to a saucepan and bring to the boil. Leave to simmer for 2–3 minutes.

🌶 Pack the chillies into the jar and add 1 tsp of salt. Slice the garlic clove as thinly as you can and add that to the jar. If you wanted to experiment and add some extras – such as oregano, lime peel, peppercorns or bay leaves – now would be the time to do so.

🌶 Pour your vinegar mixture into the jar and make sure it reaches the rim. Stir the contents of the jar to remove any air bubbles and seal the lid tightly.

🌶 You can open the jar and consume your chillies whenever you like, but it's worth playing the long game for fuller flavour and heat. Leave them for a month or two to really get the benefit of your pickling prowess. Your jar of chillies will keep in a cool, dark cupboard for up to a year. Once opened, it's best to consume them within about 10 weeks.

🌶 Turn to page 100 to find out how to make quick pickled chillies, for when you need a quicker fix.

Smoke 'em out

While thinner chillies are ideal for drying, if you have an abundance of chunkier varieties you might want to think about trying your hand at smoking them. Smoked chillies will bring a wonderful flavour to anything you add them to, so although this is a lengthier preservation technique, you will thank yourself when you're enjoying dish after dish of smoky chilli goodness.

YOU WILL NEED:

A charcoal barbecue with a lid
Kindling or newspaper
Charcoal
Wood chips for smoking (these come in a variety of "flavours")
Ripe but robust chillies of the chunkier variety

Arrange your chillies on lined baking trays and place in an oven at 100°C (210°F). Check these after half an hour – you want them to be dry but still with some flexibility.

- Soak the wood chips in water. This will slow down their burning time and ensure that they produce plenty of smoke – that's what we're here for!

- Half-fill the barbecue with charcoal and light it using some kindling or newspaper. Once it's burning nicely and there are no flames, use some tongs to separate the charcoal so there is a gap in the middle of the barbecue.

- Cover the charcoal with the wood chips and arrange the chillies on the grill above the gap in the charcoal to avoid them being cooked.

- Put the lid on the barbecue and allow a little air in through the vents. Leave for 3–4 hours, checking regularly and adding more charcoal and wood chips as needed.

- Remove from the grill and allow your chillies to cool on a rack. Store in jars, freeze or crush, and enjoy a smokier heat in your chilli-fuelled dishes.

- Cutting your chillies in half will speed up the smoking process, if you have a grill with narrower gaps so they won't fall through.

FIERY FACT

THE LONGEST CHILLI PEPPER IN THE WORLD WAS A JOE'S LONG CAYENNE GROWN BY JÜRG WIESLI IN SWITZERLAND, CLOCKING IN AT A WHOPPING 50.5 CM LONG (20 IN.). THE TITLE WAS AWARDED IN 2018 BY THE GREAT PUMPKIN COMMONWEALTH, WHICH SETS THE STANDARD IN COMPETITIVE GARDENING, AND WAS RECOGNIZED BY GUINNESS WORLD RECORDS.

Spicy oil at the ready

Chilli oil is perfect for drizzling over salads, pizzas, roasted veg – you name it. If you'd like to make your own with the fruits of your green-fingered labour, it's important to follow the instructions very carefully. Chilli oil should only be made using dried chillies. This information is vital as fresh chillies simply don't keep in oil and will start to rot. This, in turn, invites bacteria, so make sure you've dried your chillies first!

To make your own oil you will need a sterilized bottle, a few dried chillies, some chilli flakes (1 tbsp or more) and enough olive oil to fill the receptacle you're using. The more chilli you add to the oil, the hotter the end product. Pierce the chillies (this allows the oil in) and place them in a pan with the flakes and the oil. Heat gently for 5 minutes before pouring into the bottle. Shake well and store in a cupboard for a few weeks. Give it a good shake every now and then during this time and before use.

Chillies to the rescue

There are other ways to use your delicious crop other than simply eating it. If you're a keen gardener, you'll be pleased to learn that chillies can be used as a natural pesticide. This easy chilli spray will repel lots of insects and garden pests.

YOU WILL NEED:

8–10 chillies
1 litre water
2 drops washing-up liquid

Chop the chillies roughly and, along with the seeds, mix into 1 litre boiled water. Add the washing-up liquid – be careful to only add two drops. Leave the mixture to cool, cover and place in a cool space for 24 hours.

Strain the mixture into spray bottles, label them clearly and, *voila*. Pests, begone!

FIERY FACT

TABASCO HOT SAUCE IS DISTRIBUTED IN 185 COUNTRIES AROUND THE WORLD, WITH LABELS PRINTED IN 22 DIFFERENT LANGUAGES AND DIALECTS.

String along tradition

If you'd like to combine preservation with decoration, why not try your hand at a chilli ristra? This is an attractive arrangement of chillies on a string, which is hung up to air-dry. The ristra originated in South America, where it was used to preserve surplus chillies while also providing decoration. You will need plenty of thin, pointy chillies for this – think cayenne or similar as these will dry in less time than beefier varieties. Use several different colours for a more vibrant decoration.

Take a tapestry needle and some black thread. Tie a large knot at one end of the thread, attach the needle, then simply sew through each chilli stem, alternating the chillies so that they point to the left and right. When your final chilli is on the string, tie a loop at the top and hang your ristra in a warm spot in your home.

Allow the chillies to dry and simply help yourself whenever your culinary creations need a kick.

THIS IS THE KIND OF PLANT
THAT ENDEARS ITSELF TO
A TEENAGE BOY. THESE
WEREN'T VEGETABLES, THEY
WERE WEAPONS! AND IT WAS
LEGAL TO GROW THEM.

JAMES GORMAN

Competitive chilli consumption

As the superhot chilli pepper has become more prevalent, so chilli-eating competitions have become increasingly popular. Evolved from the Texan chilli con carne cook-offs of the 1940s, these contests are more a case of chilli-eating competitors sitting in a row, munching and sweating – and possibly crying – while a crowd looks on and gawps.

The world's number-one chilli-eating champion is West Londoner Shahina Waseem, who has chowed down on the hottest varieties in the world all in the name of fiery glory – and won a staggering 81 chilli-eating contests. She claims to have overdone it before, competing in one too many competitions in close succession, testing both her taste buds and her tolerance for heartburn, but maintains that her tried-and-tested techniques see her through. She swears by a pre-competition peanut butter and banana sandwich to line her stomach and says Babybel cheese and chocolate milk sort her out afterwards.

Chilli festivals and events take place all over the world. One of the biggest originated in El Paso, Texas, in 1988. The National Fiery Foods Show is something of a Mecca for chilli heads and is still hosted by its founder, Dave DeWitt, known as the Pope of Peppers to his friends. The festival now takes place in Albuquerque, New Mexico, and hosts the Scovie Awards each year – which is like the Oscars for hot sauce.

Chillies offering protection

We know that the Mayans used to burn rows of chillies to create a burning smokescreen to ward off their enemies, but what about chillies as a protective measure in modern times? The most well-known is pepper spray, which causes an incredibly unpleasant burning sensation against the skin. When sprayed in the face, it forces the eyes to close, rendering the person on the receiving end temporarily blind. And the active ingredient in pepper spray? Why, capsaicin, of course – and its Scoville rating can clock in at 5 million (approximately two and a half times stronger than the Carolina Reaper). The spray was originally produced for use in the USA as protection for when faced with a bear, cougar or wolf, but has since been used on humans. For instance, pepper spray is sometimes used by the police against assailants and to control rioters, and in some countries can be purchased and carried for self-defence – although it is illegal in the UK.

Military scientists in India have used the million-Scoville-busting ghost pepper (bhut jolokia) to create a "chilli grenade" to help with crowd control in severe situations. The non-lethal weapon works in a similar way to tear gas, causing all those in its wake to run for cover with their eyes streaming and burning before they become incapacitated.

Chillies, health and well-being

In the days before medicine and refrigeration, chillies were particularly useful due to their ability to repel microbes. Chillies were a godsend, especially in the tropics where food was susceptible to bacteria and swift spoiling, as they can kill up to 75 per cent of these nasties. Research has found strong links between historic chilli consumption and proximity to the equator – even overriding the relationship between consumption and growing conditions – implying that those living in tropical climates were actually using chillies as a life-preserving ingredient.

Creams, balms and patches containing capsaicin and cayenne are sold in natural health settings, designed to warm the muscles and ease aches and pains. Capsaicin cream has been found to be effective at reducing arthritic pain, as well as muscle strains, sprains and even migraines. These creams work by affecting the neurotransmitter that alerts the brain to any discomfort, reducing the perception of the pain.

CHILLI IS MUCH IMPROVED BY HAVING HAD A DAY TO CONTEMPLATE ITS FATE.

JOHN STEELE GORDON

COOKING
WITH CHILLIES

Chillies might have a variety of uses, but, for most people, their flavour and firepower is there to be enjoyed. From condiments such as chilli chutney and quick pickled peppers, to fiery showstoppers such as classic chilli, traditional tacos and spicy pasta, to desserts and hot cocktails, there are so many ways to enjoy chillies. Whether you're looking for a weeknight meal with a kick or want to wow your guests, this chapter is full of recipe ideas to whet your appetite. Do you dare turn up the heat? It's time to set your taste buds alight!

Conversions and measurements

The recipes in this chapter use metric measurements, but if you prefer using imperial (and you don't have a smartphone to do the conversions for you), here are some basic tables:

30 g ≈ 1 oz	15 ml ≈ 0.5 fl. oz
60 g ≈ 2 oz	30 ml ≈ 1 fl. oz
85 g ≈ 3 oz	75 ml ≈ 2.5 fl. oz
115 g ≈ 4 oz	120 ml ≈ 4 fl. oz
255 g ≈ 9 oz	270 ml ≈ 9 fl. oz

Cooking with Chillies:

CONDIMENTS

Quick pickled chillies

Keep a jar of these in the fridge to sprinkle on salads, pizzas, nachos and tacos.

Makes enough to fill a 500-ml jar

INGREDIENTS

Enough chillies or peppers of your choice to loosely fill the jar (approx. 400 g)

2 large cloves garlic, minced

125 ml cider vinegar

125 ml water

65 g sugar

1 tsp mustard seeds

1 tsp coriander seeds

Slice your chillies thinly. Make sure the jar is sterilized and still warm, then add the chillies and the crushed garlic.

Place the rest of the ingredients in a saucepan and gently bring to the boil until the sugar has dissolved.

Pour the hot liquid over the chillies and secure the lid. Allow the contents to cool to room temperature and then transfer to the fridge, where they will keep for around three months if unopened. Once opened, consume within a couple of weeks.

Sweet chilli beetroot chutney

This is delicious with cheese and crackers or as an addition to any sandwich.

Makes enough to fill a small jar

INGREDIENTS

2 small beetroots, cooked and grated
6 tbsp sugar
2 tbsp white wine vinegar
2 tsp crushed chillies
2 tsp cumin seeds
Salt to taste

Add all ingredients to a saucepan and cook over a medium heat until the sugar has dissolved. Cook further if required to achieve desired consistency. Transfer to warm, sterilized jar and allow to cool if not eating immediately. Will keep in the fridge for up to a week.

Fermented salsa

Make your own restaurant-grade salsa while doing something good for your gut. It takes time, but it's definitely worth it.

Makes enough to fill a 1-litre jar

INGREDIENTS

400 g cherry tomatoes, chopped
1 white onion, chopped
1 red chilli (adjust according to your preference/ tolerance)
3 cloves garlic, minced
½ bunch fresh coriander, chopped
1 lime, juiced
1 tsp sea salt
½ tsp cracked black pepper
A fermentation weight, lettuce/cabbage leaf or half a pepper

Ahead of making your salsa, be sure to sterilize your jar. In a large bowl, add all the ingredients apart from the fermentation weight and mix well. Test the mixture to make sure you can taste the salt. If you cannot, add a little more until you can. The salt shouldn't be overpowering, but it is key to the fermentation process, so don't skip this stage.

Pour the mixture into your jar, making sure all the juice makes it out of the bowl and into the jar. Push the salsa down to make sure it is fully submerged.

Use the fermentation weight (or lettuce/cabbage leaf or half a pepper) to weigh down the salsa mixture to keep it below the liquid level. Then seal the jar tightly.

Place the jar in a cool place in your kitchen out of direct sunlight. After 24 hours you should see bubbles beginning to form as the salsa begins to live and breathe. Open the jar briefly to "burp" it and then reseal for another 24 hours. Taste the salsa and add extra seasoning if required. When it is to your liking, transfer the jar to the fridge.

TOP TIP: This salsa will keep for up to two months in the fridge. Due to its prep time, you might want to double the above ingredients in order to produce a bigger batch.

Quick chilli sauce

Why not try your hand at creating your very own chilli sauce? This is easily adaptable, so you can adjust it to suit your heat tolerance.

Makes enough to fill a 500-ml jar

INGREDIENTS

1 tin cherry tomatoes
1 tbsp tomato puree
1 chilli (the hotter the better)
1 white onion, chopped
2 cloves garlic, minced
1 tbsp vinegar
Salt and pepper to taste

Simply add the ingredients to a blender and blend until it reaches the desired consistency. Transfer to a sterilized jar and store in the fridge for up to two weeks, or freeze portions in an ice-cube tray to have on hand to add to sauces, soups, stews or chilli con carne.

Cooking with Chillies:

STARTERS, SIDES AND MAINS

Chilli cheese fries

The ultimate in warming, spicy comfort food – don't scrimp on the toppings.

Serves 4

INGREDIENTS

See page 112 for the chilli recipe and either halve it or make the full amount and prepare for leftovers

1 kg potatoes
200 g cheddar cheese, grated
Sunflower oil
2 avocados, smashed
¼ bunch coriander, chopped
150 g soured cream
Picked jalapeños or fresh chillies, as desired

Preheat oven to 200°C (400°F) and prepare your chilli as per the recipe on page 112.

To make the fries, first soak the potatoes in hot water for half an hour. Peel if you prefer, but skin-on fries are also delicious. Drain the potatoes and make sure they are dry before proceeding.

Slice the potatoes into sticks about ½ cm wide and place in a bowl. Drizzle over the oil, shake the potato sticks and drizzle over more oil to coat. Place on greaseproof paper on a baking tray and put in oven for 20 minutes.

Once the fries are cooked, serve on four different heat-safe plates, top with plenty of chilli, add a handful of cheese and place under the grill until cheese is bubbling.

Remove from grill and add your toppings – smashed avocado, soured cream, chillies and coriander – as desired.

Padrón peppers

Hot, blistered Padrón peppers are delicious as a starter or a snack – take a bite, close your eyes and transport yourself to a tapas bar in the Spanish sunshine.

INGREDIENTS

Olive oil
Padrón peppers (any amount!)
Coarse sea salt

Add a good glug of olive oil to a frying pan on a high heat and allow it to start smoking. Add the Padrón peppers and allow them to blister on one side. Shake the pan to flip the peppers around so they blister evenly.

Cook for a few minutes, moving the peppers around as necessary until they are blistered all over and browning. Remove from the heat, transfer to a bowl and sprinkle over salt before serving.

Roasted butternut squash and chilli soup

This one will warm your soul on a winter's day.

Serves 4

INGREDIENTS

1 butternut squash
1 medium onion
2 cloves garlic, minced
1 chilli, deseeded and chopped
1 litre vegetable stock
Handful fresh coriander (optional)
1 chilli, sliced (optional)

Preheat your oven to 200°C (400°F) and place the butternut squash on a baking tray. Make a few incisions in the squash and place in the oven for an hour or until it starts to brown and feels soft. Remove from oven. Once cool, remove the seeds and skin from the butternut squash and cut into manageable pieces.

Add a little oil to a large pan and cook the onion until it begins to soften. Add the garlic and chilli and cook for one minute. Add the butternut squash and mix. Next, add the vegetable stock and simmer for 15 minutes. Season to taste.

Use a hand blender to obtain desired consistency and serve immediately. Scatter fresh coriander and thinly sliced chillies on top if you choose.

Tomato and chilli pasta

The perfect dinner when time is tight.

Serves 4

INGREDIENTS

Olive oil

1 large onion,
   chopped

3 cloves garlic, minced

1 large red chilli,
   deseeded and chopped

500 g passata

1 tsp dried oregano

1 tsp dried basil

250 g linguini or
   spaghetti

Add a good glug of olive oil to a pan and cook the onion on a medium heat until it starts to soften. Add the garlic and chilli and cook for another minute.

Pour in the passata and add the oregano and basil. Cook on a medium heat for around 10 minutes or until the sauce starts to thicken. Turn the heat right down and set to one side.

Cook the pasta of your choice as per the instructions on the packet. Drain and add to the pan containing the sauce. Mix them together well and serve immediately.

Chilli con/non carne

An absolute classic, totally versatile, loved by many. It's worth making a big batch of this recipe and freezing it for quick weeknight suppers.

Serves 6

INGREDIENTS

Olive oil

2 onions, chopped

2 cloves garlic, minced

2 red peppers, chopped

1 red chilli (optional; this will raise the heat levels somewhat)

400 g tin black beans

400 g tin kidney beans

2 x 400 g tins chopped tomatoes

500 g minced beef or vegan mince (or omit this altogether and add another tin of different beans, chickpeas or sweetcorn)

1 tsp hot chilli powder, heaped

1 tsp ground cumin, heaped

½ stock cube

1 avocado, smashed (optional)

Soured cream (optional)

Grated cheese to serve

Pour a glug of oil to a large pan over a medium-high heat and add the onions. Cook until they begin to soften. Add the garlic, red peppers and chilli (if using), and cook for 2 minutes. If using vegan mince, add this as well.

Drain the beans and add to the pan along with the chopped tomatoes. Fill up a tin with water and add that too. Now, if using minced beef, add it to the pan and break it up with a wooden spoon.

Add the chilli powder, cumin and stock cube and bring the mixture to the boil. Then lower the heat and allow the chilli to bubble away gently for an hour. Check on it occasionally, give it a stir and adjust the heat if it's getting too lively. Add a little water if it has reduced too much.

Serve on its own or with rice, topped with avocado, soured cream and cheese, as you desire.

Sweet potato and black bean tacos

These tacos are delicious and don't require much effort to put together.

Serves 4

INGREDIENTS

2 large sweet potatoes, chopped into cubes
½ tsp smoked paprika
½ tsp dried cumin
½ tsp dried chilli flakes
½ small onion, chopped
400 g tinned black beans
8 corn or wheat tortillas
1 avocado, chopped
1 leaf red cabbage, chopped
Chilli sauce (optional)

You can either roast the sweet potatoes for a crisper taco filling or boil them for a wetter one – you decide! If you choose to roast, preheat oven to 200°C (400°F). Place the sweet potato on a baking tray drizzled with olive oil and sprinkled with the spices. Bake for 25 minutes.

If you prefer a wetter taco filling, boil the sweet potatoes until tender, drain and set to one side.

Finely chop the onion, place in a pan over a medium heat with a little oil and cook for one minute only. Add the spices at this point if you boiled the potatoes.

Drain the black beans and add them to the pan along with the sweet potato. Cook over a medium heat, stirring frequently until the beans are warmed through.

Divide the mixture between the tortillas and top with avocado and red cabbage – and don't forget the chilli sauce!

Sausage and chilli bake

This is a quick and simple dinner to warm the soul. Serve on its own, with sourdough bread or with a side, such as rice or a baked or mashed potato.

Serves 4

INGREDIENTS

8 sausages (meat or vegan)

1 large red onion

1 green or red pepper

Olive oil

2 tsp cumin seeds

400 g tin cherry tomatoes

400 g tin black beans (or whatever kind of beans you have in the cupboard)

200 ml red wine

125 ml vegetable stock

1 tsp oregano

2 tsp chilli powder

½ tsp smoked paprika

Fresh coriander (optional)

Chopped chillies (optional)

Preheat the oven to 200°C (400°C) and start prepping. Toss the sausages, onion and pepper together in a roasting tin with a good glug of olive oil and the cumin seeds. Cook for 20–25 minutes, keeping an eye on the sausages – when they start to brown, move to the next step. (If using vegan sausages, cook according to packet – you might need to start the veg roasting and add the sausages after 10 minutes, for example.)

Add the tomatoes, beans, wine, stock, and herbs and spices to the tray and give it a good stir. Cook for 20 minutes or until the sauce has become nice and thick.

Sprinkle chopped coriander or fresh chillies on top as desired.

Cooking with Chillies:

DESSERTS

Chocolate chilli cheesecake

A dinner-party-worthy spicy showstopper.

Serves 10

INGREDIENTS

12 digestive biscuits
55 g butter, melted
120 g caster sugar (plus 1 tbsp for the base)
175 g dark chocolate
200 g full-fat cream cheese
½ tsp chilli powder
125 ml double cream
1 tbsp cocoa powder
Chilli flakes or fresh chillies to garnish

Grease and line an 18 cm (7 in.) cake tin – springform is best so you can easily release the cheesecake once it's ready.

Crush the biscuits to a fine crumb and combine with 1 tbsp sugar and the butter. Then pour this mixture into the cake tin and press down firmly. Put in the fridge to harden for 30 minutes – or an hour if you have the luxury of time.

Melt the chocolate in the microwave or in a heat-proof bowl over a pan of hot water, and set aside to cool a little. Combine the cream cheese, sugar and chilli powder in a small bowl, and also set to one side. In another bowl, whip the cream until peaks form, then fold in the cocoa powder. Once combined, fold in the cream and sugar mixtures and the melted chocolate.

Remove your biscuit base from the fridge and pour the cheesecake mixture into the tin. Place in the freezer for 2 hours. Allow it to rest at room temperature for 30 minutes before serving. Scatter over sliced fresh chillies or chilli flakes for decoration, as you wish.

Vegan chocolate chilli brownies

These squares of spicy chocolate joy will blow your mind.

Makes 16

INGREDIENTS

200 g dark chocolate
170 g self-raising flour
180 g sugar
1 tsp chilli flakes
1 large red chilli, chopped
230 ml plant milk of your choice
75 ml vegetable or sunflower oil

Preheat the oven to 180°C (350°F) and grease and line a square baking tin.

Take 150 g of the chocolate and set the rest to one side. Melt the chocolate using a bain-marie – place the chocolate in a heat-proof bowl, then place the bowl over a pan of simmering water. Stir the chocolate until it has melted.

Combine the flour, sugar, chilli flakes and chopped chilli in a bowl. Stir in the milk, oil and melted chocolate until well mixed.

Smash the unmelted chocolate into chunks and stir into the mixture. Pour the whole lot into the tin and bake in oven for 20–25 minutes. You want the brownies to be firm on the outside but gooey in the middle.

Remove from the oven and leave to cool for 10 minutes. Then turn out on to a cooling rack and serve while still warm.

Cooking with Chillies:

DRINKS

Chilli mojito

Spice up your cocktails with a bit of help from the chilli pepper.

Serves 1

INGREDIENTS
3 slices fresh red chilli
Crushed ice
50 ml white rum
10 ml fresh lime juice
15 ml sugar syrup
Soda water

Place the chilli at the bottom of a highball glass and bruise it with a spoon to release the flavours. Half-fill the glass with crushed ice, and add the rum, lime juice and sugar syrup. Give it all a good stir.

Add more crushed ice if desired and top up the drink with soda water. Add a wedge of lime and more slices of chilli to garnish if you feel the need for more heat.

"Clean" jalapeño margarita

This cocktail combines the best of Mexico in one glass.

Serves 1

INGREDIENTS

2–3 slices fresh jalapeño
Crushed ice
60 ml tequila blanco
25 ml fresh lime juice
10 ml sugar syrup

Place the jalapeño slices in a glass and bruise them with a spoon to release the flavours. Add a good amount of crushed ice and pour over the tequila, lime juice and sugar syrup. Stir very well. (Alternatively, shake it in a cocktail shaker if you have one.)

Top with more crushed ice if desired and even more slices of jalapeño if you're asking for trouble.

Conclusion

If you've made it this far, chances are you are craving something fiery, whether that's a steaming bowl of chilli accompanied by a spicy margarita or a plate of nachos smothered in the hottest hot sauce you can lay your hands on. Or perhaps your green fingers are now itching to get growing some of the more unusual varieties of chilli we talked about on these pages. Either way, remember the golden rule – always have some milk in the fridge or vanilla ice cream in the freezer to cool you down. Variety, as they say, is the spice of life and that is especially true when it comes to the mighty chilli pepper. Best wishes in your heat-seeking endeavours – go forth and continue your chilli quest.

Resources

BOOKS

- Lynes, Andy *How to Be a Chilli Head: Inside the Red-Hot World of the Chilli Cult* (2015, Portico)
- Maguire, Kay *Red Hot Chilli Grower: The Complete Guide to Planting, Picking and Preserving Chillies* (2015, Quid)
- Floyd, David *The Hot Book of Chillies* (2006, New Holland)

WEBSITES

- Worldofchillies.com
- Thechileman.org
- Chillisgalore.co.uk
- Chillipepperpete.com

VIDEO AND AUDIO

- *The Science of Spiciness* – TED-Ed video by Rose Eveleth (YouTube)
- *It Burns* – podcast series with Marc Fennell (available on Audible)
- *Craft Hot Sauce* – podcast series

Have you enjoyed this book?
If so, find us on Facebook at
SUMMERSDALE PUBLISHERS, on Twitter at
@SUMMERSDALE and on Instagram at
@SUMMERSDALEBOOKS and get in touch.
We'd love to hear from you!

WWW.SUMMERSDALE.COM